This Coloring Book Belongs to......

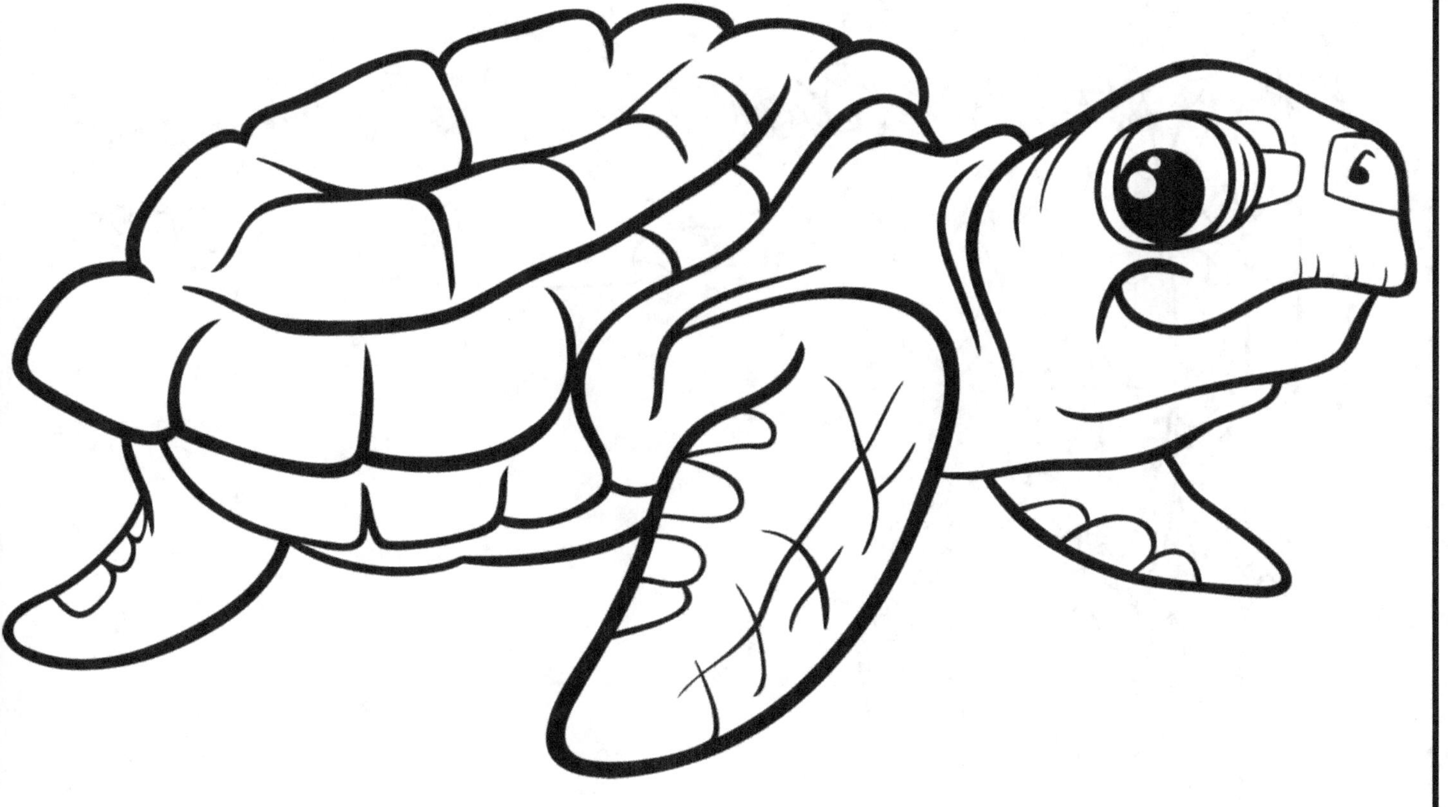

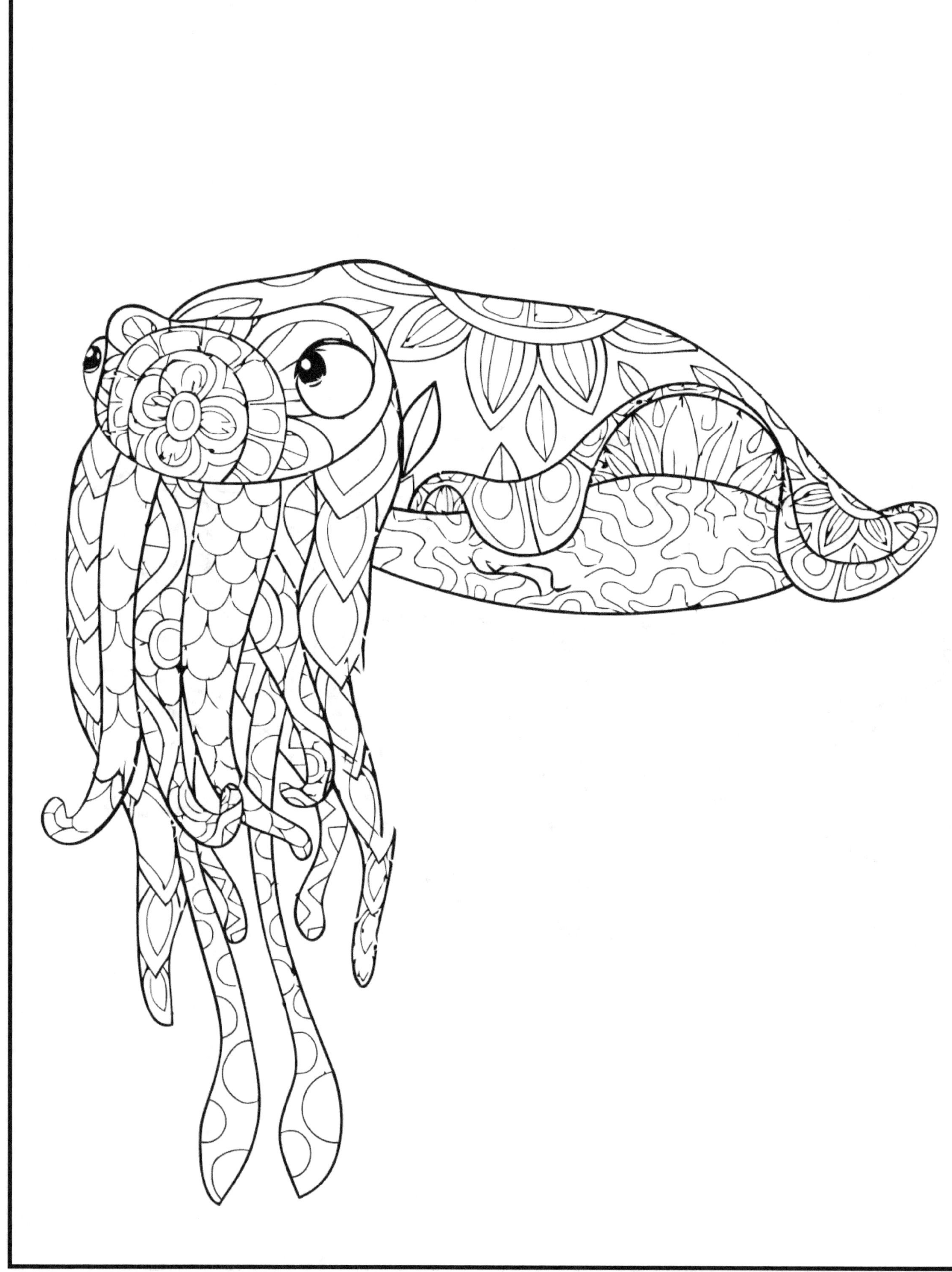

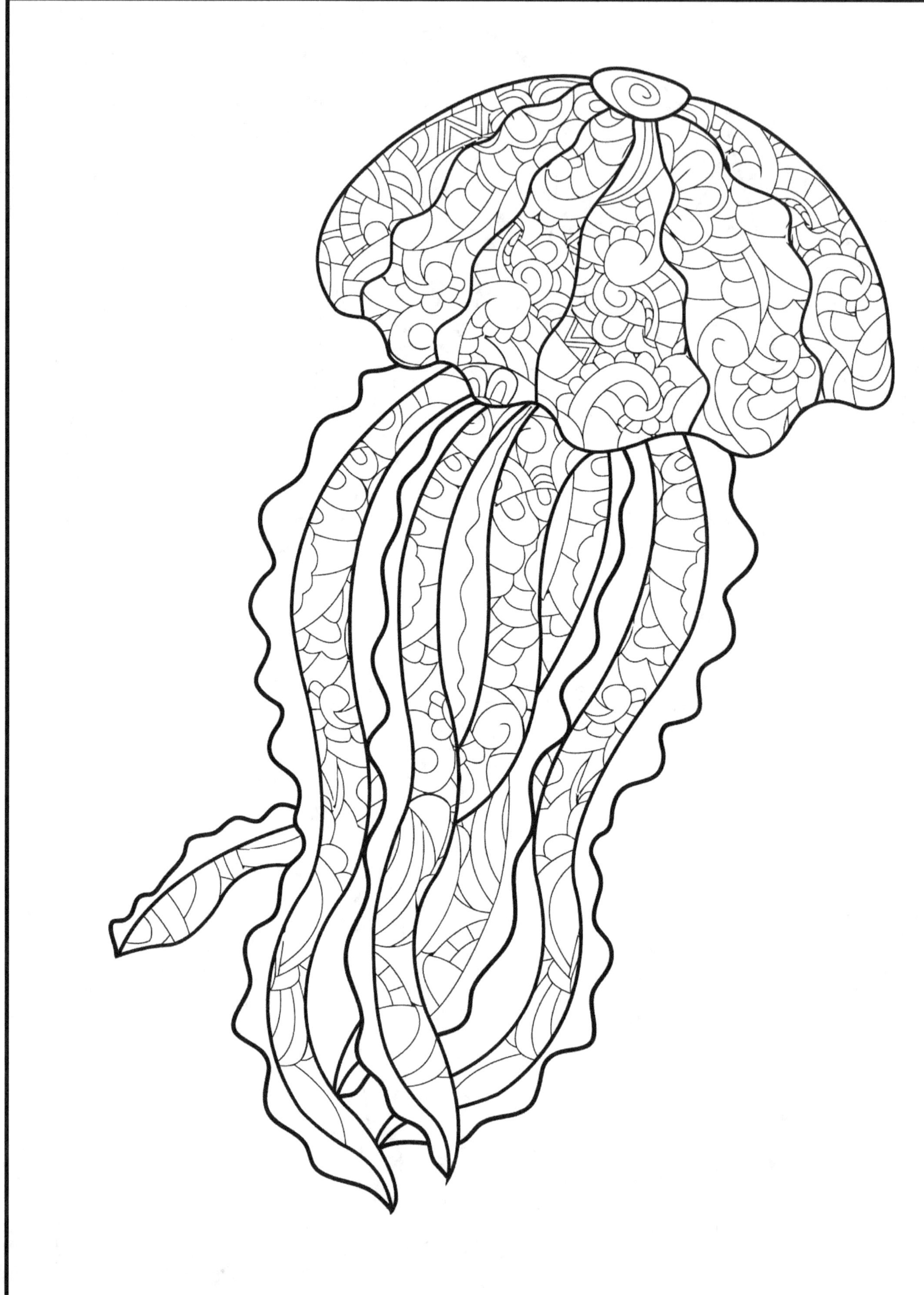

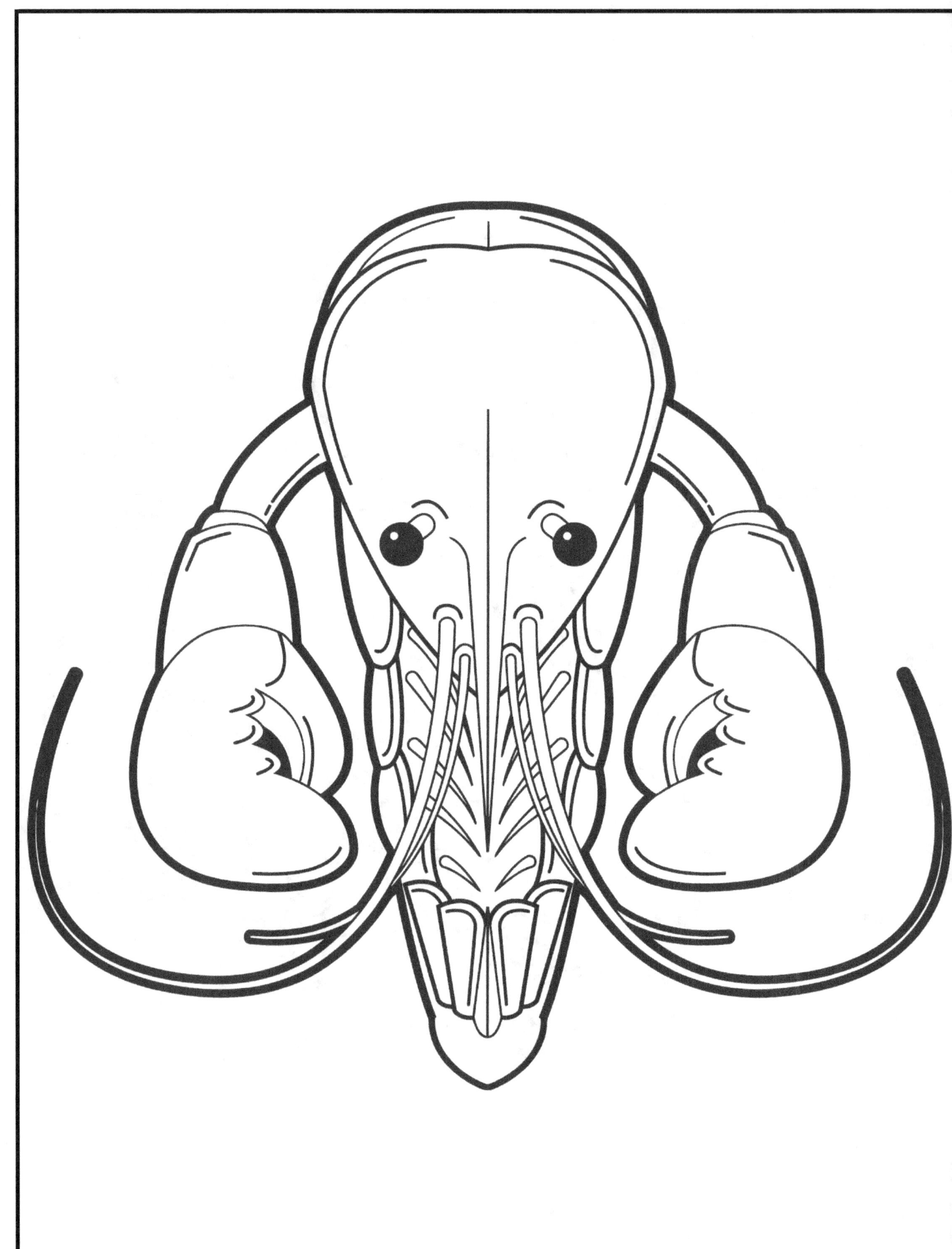

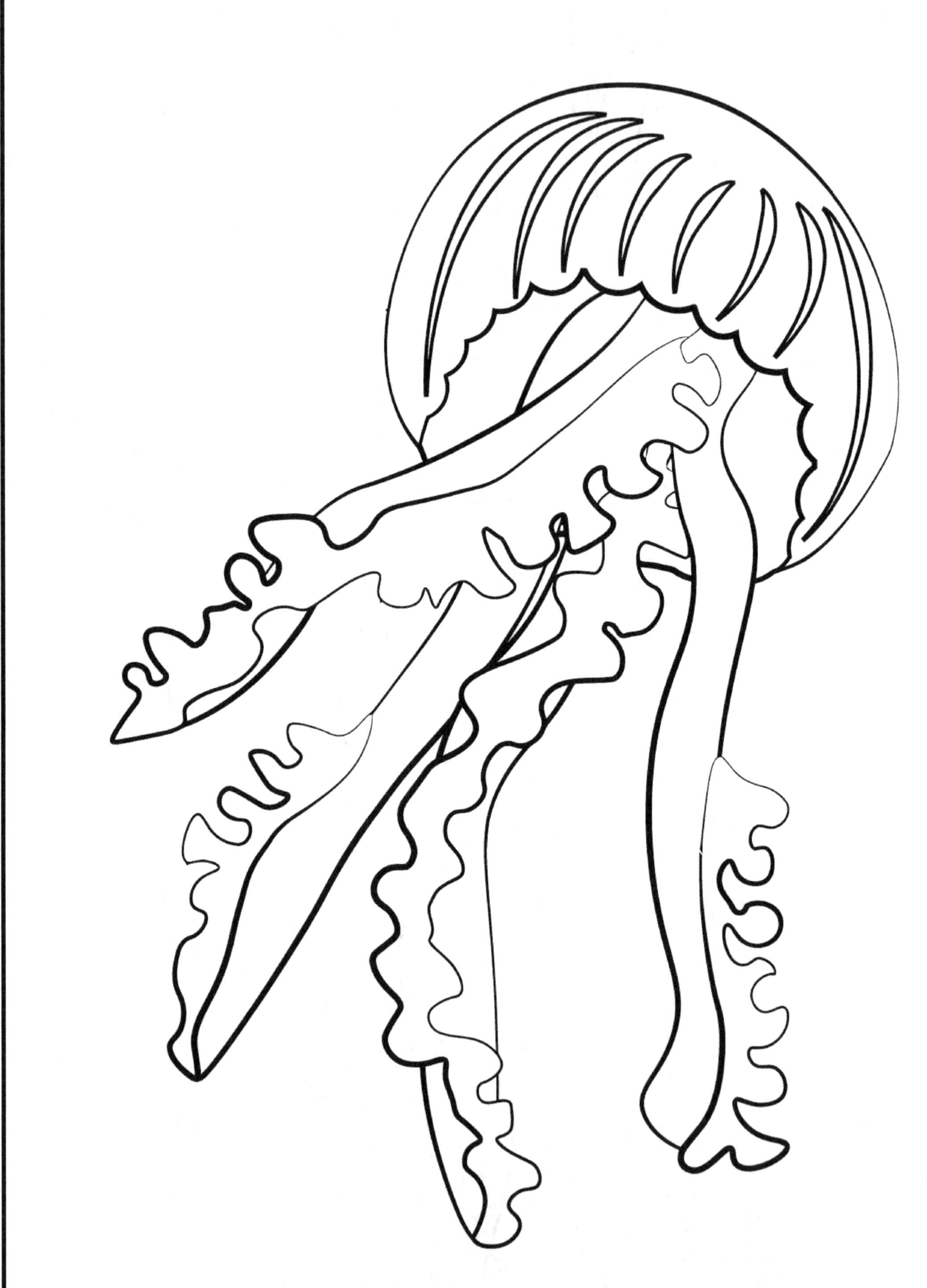

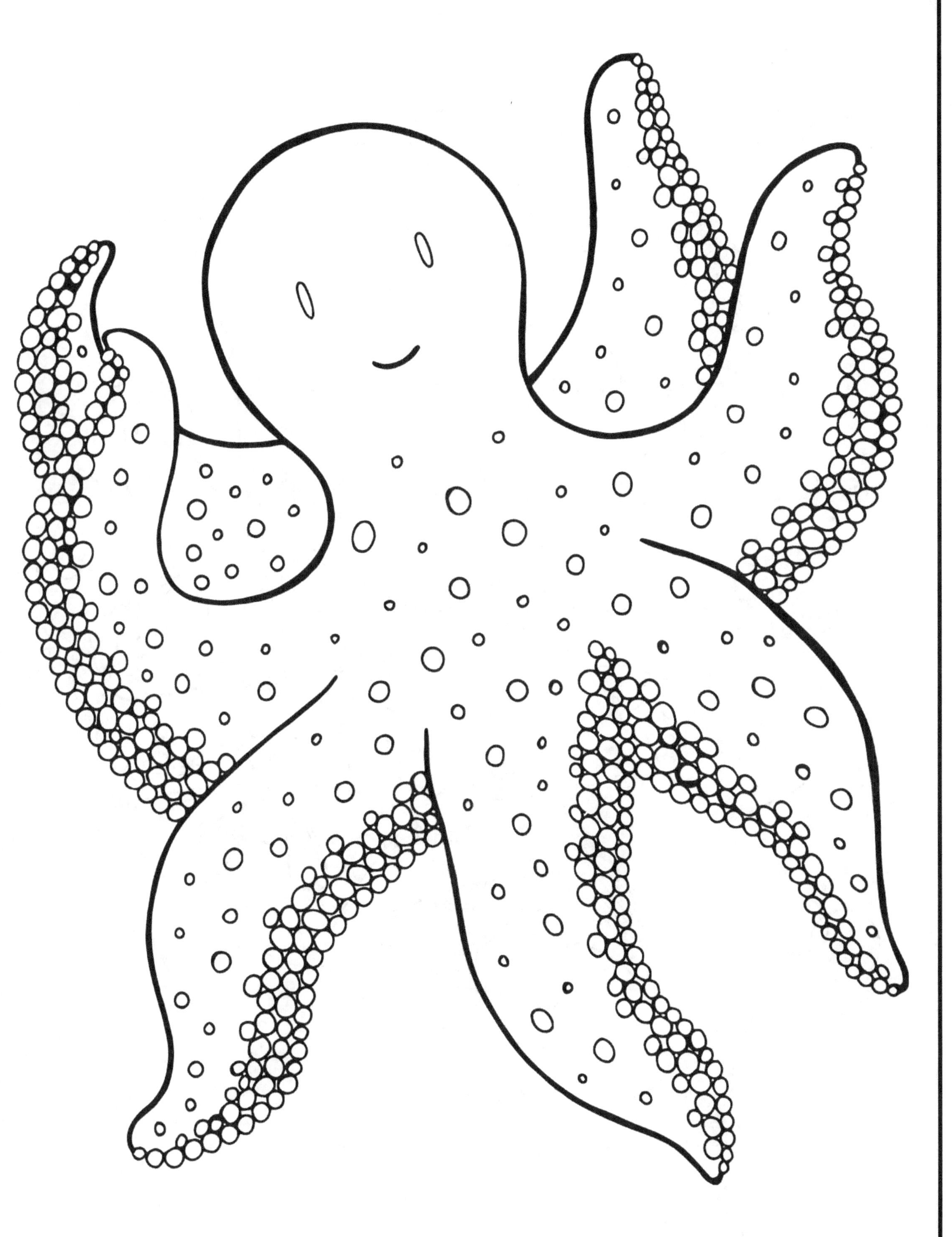

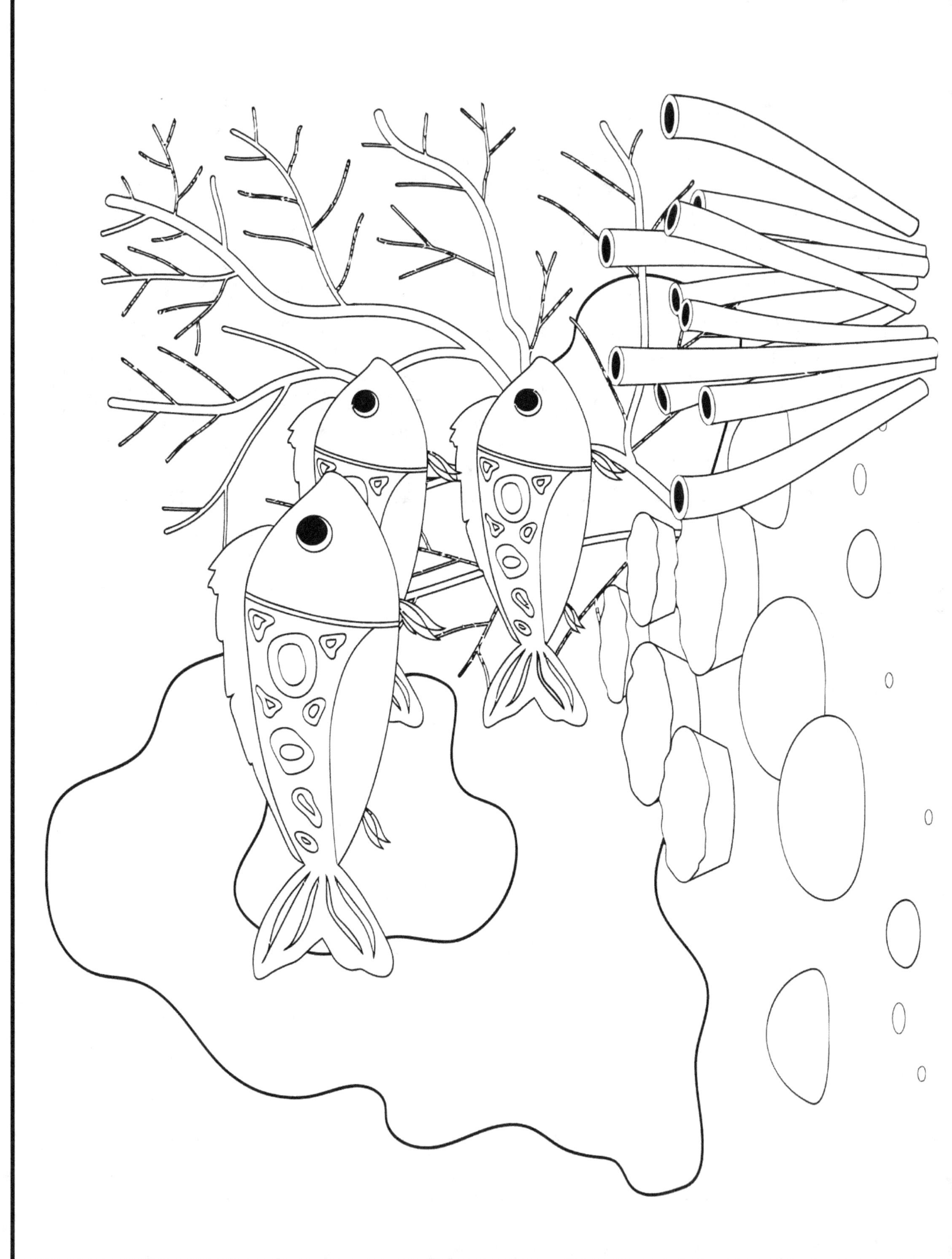

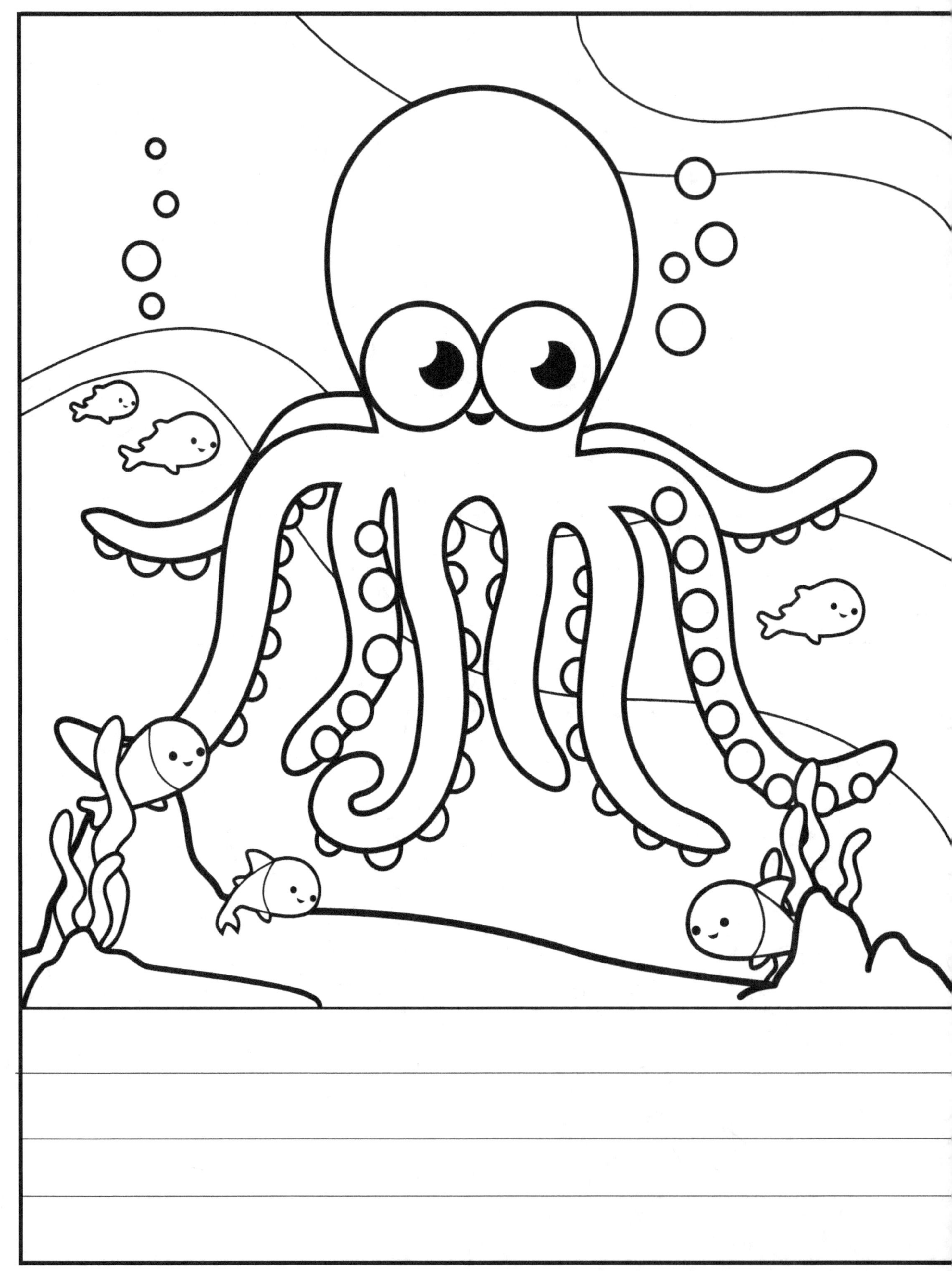

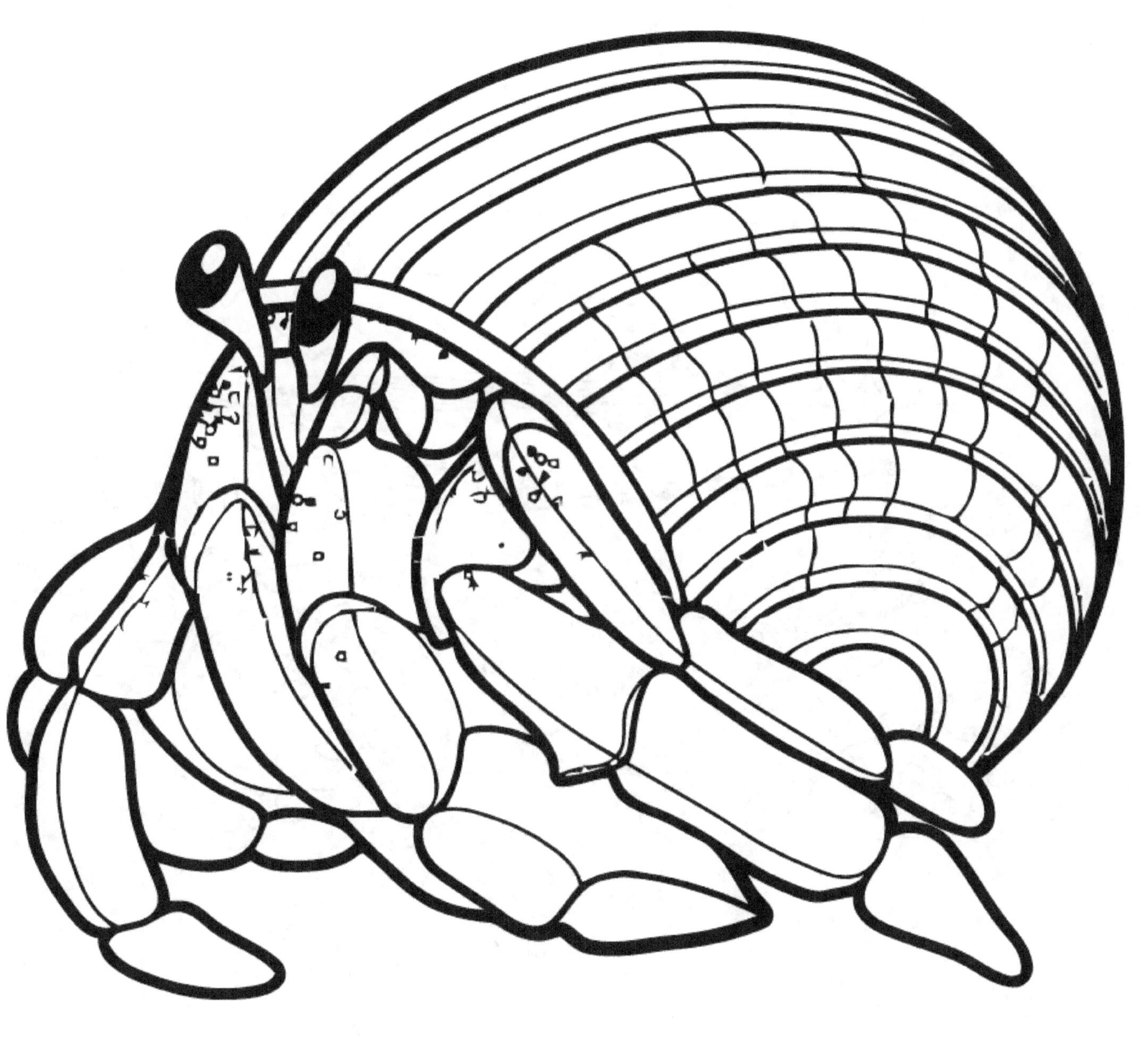

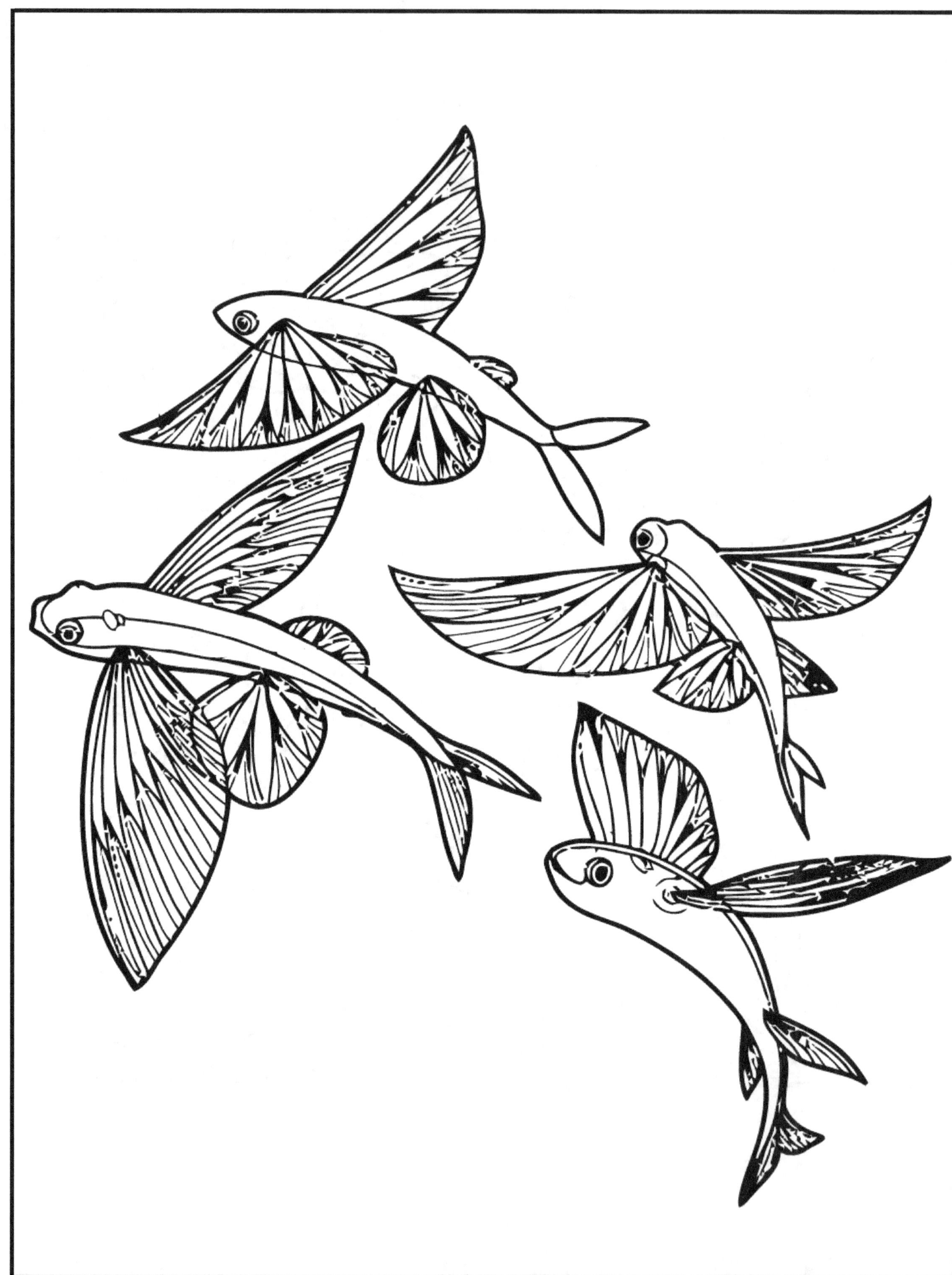

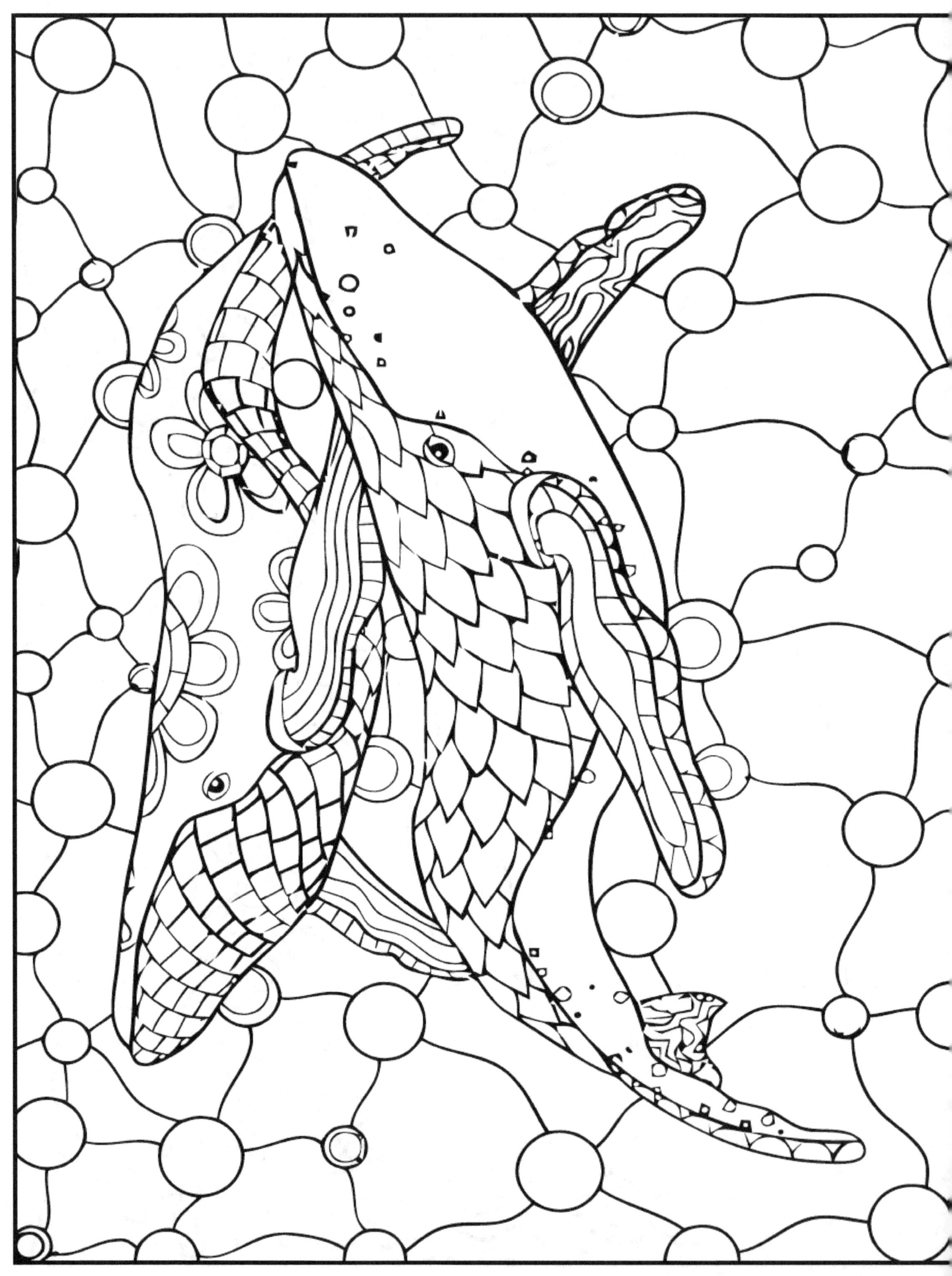

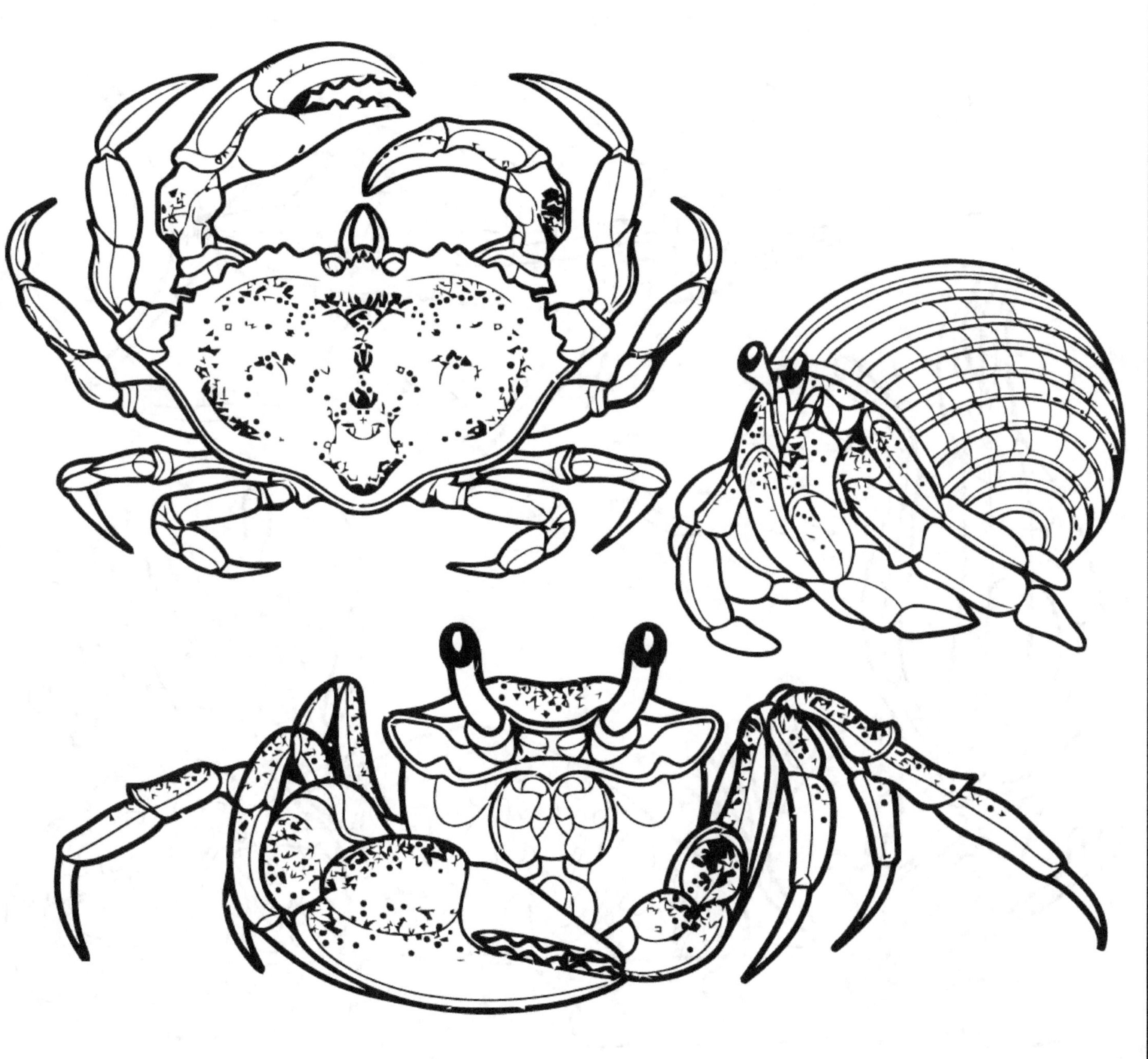